# The Remains of Yesterday



Nooriya Yaqub

BookLeaf Publishing

Presentation by *BookLeaf Publishing*

Web: www.bookleafpub.com

E-mail: info@bookleafpub.com

ISBN: 9789357212670

First edition 2023

*For me.*

*But you can read it too.*

# ACKNOWLEDGEMENT

I would like to thank myself for going ahead with writing this book. It was really difficult for me to tap into old feelings of my past when writing these poems, but it was important for me to heal, and finally let go of the things I was holding onto that were no longer good for me.

I also wanted to write this book to help others in that process. To allow others to let go and grow if they have faced any experiences written in this book.

I also would like to thank all my friends for loving all the pieces they read of mine and to keep inspiring me to continue writing, even when I feel what I am writing is not always good enough.

I would like to thank my best friends, Jannat & Saman, for always being there for me. Without their continued support, I do not think I would have kept writing.

Finally, I would like to thank the most important people in my life, my family, for always

encouraging me to talk about how I feel and to never feel like I should hide that.
I am always going to be grateful to have that.

# The Rose and the Thorns

At first, you were a beautiful rose, gorgeous in
an iridescent light.
But it was only at a distance.
Only at a glance.

Eventually, you slowly became a violent storm
on the edge between chaos and insanity.
Fantasy mixed with the calmness of knowing
reality was going to bring you back to the
present.
Out of the dream you've been living.

Your love felt like being pricked by a thorn
repeatedly.
Blood leaving my body, with every second, with
every minute.
With every inch of me on the verge of fighting
against it,
And being on the line of giving in.
Giving in to the mental torment you knew I was
not prepared for.
And now my body aches from the thought of
you.

All my questions buried internally.
But all the answers are hanging in mid-air.
Floating in existence but I am now unable to
attend to those thoughts.
I do not have a choice.
But you chose not to revisit the unwanted
visitors inside your mind,
In the place you once called home.
Now it's just a place you don't belong in.
You just feel alone there.

But I always have to face the agonising silence
of your absence,
And the tantalising voices in my head.
Echoing your name.
All the conversations we had,
Your words edged inside my brain,
Like being cut with a knife.
Leaving a mark of remembrance of this tragic
event.
The one that I cannot forget.
The one where I saved someone who never
wanted to be saved.

# Left for Sorrow in an Ephemeral Thud of Sadness

An ephemeral thud of sadness echoes in my mind.
In my body. In my soul.

I cannot forget it.
I cannot forget you.
Is all I hear my mind whispering to me at 4:00 am when I cannot sleep.

I dream of you.
Even when I am awake.
Even when every part of me aches to remember what happened.
Every time my mind revisits the thoughts of you.

The thoughts of that night you were screaming.
Screaming at the wreckage.
The damage that you caused.
The damage and pain that we caused.
And the melancholy ache that is etched into your brain.

You cannot forget what they told you.
The look they gave you when they found out.

You used to run from the monsters under your bed.
But you cannot hide, you cannot escape from the ones in your head.

# Before the mirage

Take me back to that night before the mirage.
The mirage of the fantasy blurring the reality,
Where you would hold my hand and lead me to sea.
I would float in water with you swimming next to me.

Take me back to the night.
The night before I fell in love with you.
I would run as far as I could away from this town.
As far as I could away from you.
Once I could envision all the things you were about to do.

Take me back to that night I was in your room.
Lying in your sheets.
With my head resting on your chest.
As you kiss my forehead.
And I would reply, "goodnight, my love".

Take me back to that day in your car,
Where you took me to the cinema.
But all I could do was focus on you.

Like the way strands of hair would fall down your face.
I would watch you move them away
With your fingers,
That were slowly tangled in mine.
Holding me close. I could hear your heart beating.
Beating life in this moment you had with me.
All I wanted to do was watch this film of you instead.
Thoughts rushing in my head.
I never wanted to let go of you.

Now two years later, I'm not sure that I can.
Every time I watch you with someone new
I turn corners to avoid you.
But a part of me looks back.
I cannot keep my mind off you.
Even when I want to.
All I want to do now is run to a faraway island where no one knows my name.
And I will never see you again.

# Sincerely, Yours

I know you never loved me like I loved you.
Even though you manipulated me into thinking you do.
You would hate me one moment and then love me the next.
I do not know what I want from you or what you want from me.
I guess we were never really that good at communicating.
One moment we said we would be better off as friends,
Then you start kissing me, the next.
I hate how you have this control over me.
The way you would hold me close after we fought.
The way you would tell me everything was going to turn out fine.
But I knew you didn't believe it.
All the lies you sold me,
To deviate from the truth.
To avoid reflecting on your mistakes.
Deflecting all your problems.
You played me for a fool, and I believed that the game you were playing would benefit both of us.
But in reality, it never did.

It did not even benefit you.
So, what the hell were you trying to prove?
That you couldn't be alone?
You would walk out the room with someone new hooked on your arm.
Your mind running loose with thoughts
I wonder if I was even one of the many you thought of.
The worst part of loving you was that no matter what I will do, I will always be yours.
I hate every moment of being without you.
But if I did not leave,
You would take me down in the rising tide that was always going to catch you, it was inevitable.
You would let me drown.
You would kill every part of me until I was just as broken as you.
Or maybe even more.

I will always be,
Sincerely, yours.

# The Forgotten Dream

I still have dreams of the life we promised each other.
I still dream that you are still in this bed and when I turn over, you will hold me close.
I still dream about that night of our first date.
Dancing in the glow of the streetlights, as you walk me home.
You kiss me when we reach my driveway.
All I want is for you to stay.
But you say you cannot.
I watched you walk away that night.
I watched you walk away from everything we had built.
I watched you walk away from us.

Now it feels like I am living in this forgotten dream.
Our forgotten dream.
And I do not know how to wake up from it.
Or if I ever will.

# Licensed For Failure

I am just a chapter in your story,
But you were the whole book of my life.
And I hate this emptiness.
I hate the fact that I paid the price for all your mistakes and all the decisions you made.

I guess from that moment I knew I was doomed.
That I was licensed for failure in a life with you.
I hate that I was so naive, so naive about the truth.
You loved me and I loved you but in different ways.
You loved me because I was easy to use at the time.
You came and broke me in the worst way when I was the most vulnerable.
You took all my weaknesses, and you used them against me.
Like my love was just a sick, twisted game to you.
And maybe it was.
Because you've never loved or ever been loved by the people you held close.
No, they did not care about you at all.
I hate the way I feel so see through with you.

I hate that I see past all the awful things you did
and still probably do.
Making myself believe that you will change but
I know you never will.
No matter what you go through.

# Primed For Death

I will die alone.
Alone with all your kisses that still find a way to kill me like they did when you were mine.
I am losing my mind, looking for time to borrow.
To fill all my sorrow.

I am primed for death in a life with or without you.
I am falling six feet under.
I am buried with all our chaos and thunder.

I will wake up without you.
Every morning while you are probably with someone new.
Do they love you like I loved you?
Do you still miss the memories?
I do.
Do you miss me the way I miss you?

I will die alone.
Slow and painful.
Like our love.
I will try and find my way home.
Try and find a place where I belong.

Because I have been a little lost for a while now.
Without you here.

# Legacy Falling

Do I have to die to see the other side?
They say the grass is greener, but I still miss my side.
The side that made me feel like me.
I just want to know what it is like not to sleep at four am.
And wake up at four in the afternoon.
Hating myself for loving you.

Do I have to suffer to know what it's like to heal?
To be happy, to be free?
Will I heal from all the unforgettable trauma and memories that I cannot escape from?
No matter how far I run, it is not far enough.

Is it always going to be like this?
Will I always have nothing left to give?
Nothing left to offer to you.
To anyone.
To myself.
There is nothing left to say, so I will let all the unspoken words float in the wind.
And I would watch them drift away.

I do not know what I am running away from,
But I am still running.
I am trying to let myself be happy.
But I am terrified all my happiness will leave me overnight.
And I will be left with emptiness for the rest of my life.
Overthinking about everything that went wrong in that moment.
Thinking if I ever really belonged here.
Thinking if there is a way, I could fix this mess.

I had so much potential in this life, but it was all wasted on you…

# Forge & the Glass

You forged your name onto my heart.
Engraved in the depths of my twisted mind.
Wrapped around your twisted mind.
I cannot seem to forget.

I cannot seem to remember how we got here.
Lying on your four poster, with my head in your lap.
And your fingers in my hair, moving a stray piece out of the way.
Telling me you loved the way I looked at that moment.
I asked if you were joking,
And you looked me in the eyes,
And told me you have never been so sure of anything before.

I remember those moments where you were delicate like glass.
Scattered across my memories.
Memories I do not want to remember.
Because now that glass has pierced my brain, my mind, my heart.
Until I'm bleeding for you.
Poisoned by the rush in my blood.
The rush of you in my veins.

You are not delicate anymore.
You are broken into a thousand pieces.
Slowly drowning me in your trainwreck.
You are not calm anymore.
You are wild, untamed like the seas,
That rises with the winds.
My darling, you are a hurricane.
And I am getting lost in the eye.
Feeling terrified of what is next.

# Built For This

You fade slowly with each fluorescent light that shines your face a bright gold.
An angel gold.
But you disguise as a devil, grinning from above.

And I watch you run from the headlights that follow you.
Into the blood moon.
Into midnight skies,
You cannot escape from it.
You cannot forget it.
All the memories drain from your soul,
With each drop that falls from the wound dripping from your head.
Blood scattered on the concrete,
Where you lay emotionless.
I just stood there, with shock and terror written on my face.
When I heard the screams,
Your screams echoing in the distance.
Breathless and gasping for air.

I thought this was the end.
The end of it all.

But I was wrong.
It had only started when I fled the scene.

Heard you survived the concussion.
Aggression seeping from your soul.
Oxygen leaves your lungs with all the life that is left in you.
Oh, wait, there was nothing to begin with.
Nothing to say goodbye to.
With all the hell you put me through.
So I will not visit your hospital room, you are there all alone.
After all I did for you, and nothing was reciprocated.
Dying with no one to save you, the doctors cannot even help you now.
It is always you against yourself, everyone gave up on you.
But I was still there when no one else was.

What are you going to do without me now?
You are all spent, all empty.
Consumed in all your memories.
All your trauma you projected on me.
But I will not be your punching bag anymore.
So, take a swing at something else.
I will not lie on the ground defenceless.
Powerless to all your power.
So, I hope you are happy now.
There is nothing left for me to give to anyone else.
You have taken everything I had.

I was never built for this life with you.
And it shows, it has taken its toll on me.
And this pain, this heartache is only growing stronger when we are apart.

# the art of dying

I guess you have mastered the art of dying.
Killing every inch of you that is left.
Until there is nothing left to live for.
Not for you, not for me.

You numb your feelings with the alcohol in your parent's basement.
You try to run from your fears that catch up with you in the dead of the night.
Unable to hide from all of them.
Your demons always find you in the end.

You get high off your pain.
You do not want to escape.
You need it like the air you breathe.
And everyone sees but you,
In this crowded room.
But to you it is empty, the only things you notice are your feelings.

You hold on to the one thing you have ever known.
Even if it makes you feel alone.
You set fire to the things that you love the most.

I watch us go up in flames, and I am only left with your ghost.

I guess you have mastered the art of killing what was already dead, like you.
Like your soul that's been crushed in two,
From everything you've had to endure.
And the emotional damage you don't want anymore.
You rip yourself to pieces.
Each one falling to the floor.
Scattered like ashes, all over your carpet.
You cannot fix this at all.

# Emotion Sickness

Sometimes I get so far in my head,
That I forget anything else exists.
I hold onto the past, past memories of us.
In this one life we had, it was never enough.
It was not enough time with you.
And too much all at once.

All I have now are thoughts I place in the
carefully constructed shelves I have in my mind.
Taking them down, into a place they do not
belong.
They do not belong in this life without you.

I ache with emotion sickness.
It enters my bloodstream.
Like oxygen.
Like I need it.
Like I crave it.
Like I cannot live without it.

Sometimes I feel like I am losing my mind.
Borrowing time I do not have.
Hours pass with each day, each night.
Wondering what is left?
What is next?
What is going to last?

You give me an emotional motion sickness I
cannot get rid of.
It is engraved in my chest, with the same knife
you had pressed against my throat,
When you let me go.

But this time it is different,
More lonely and melancholy.
More isolating in my mind.
I detach myself from everything.
Until I cannot feel anything at all.
Until I cannot feel your presence in the spaces
around me.
Until I do not remember you anymore.

# Chosen Nature

You twist my words, twist my meaning.
Twist my soul until it is all yours.
I have no self-control anymore.

You take and break more of me,
Then you were ever owed.
You vowed to change your selfish ways.
But you will always stay the same.

That is just your chosen nature.
But it is not mine.
It was never mine.
Even though you made me believe that it was.
It is insane looking back now.
How no one caught on to how twisted and cruel
you were until it was too late.
I was too late to save from the peril you inflicted
on me.

Now you are someone else's problem.
And I hope they are happy.
Because you never will be,
With all the thoughts that consume you.
You store them all on white shelves.
So, you never have to think about them.

And no one can get close to the mental torment
you put yourself through.

No, you would rather play the victim.
So, go ahead.
I will not be here to watch you lose all the games
you play,
When your rules always change.
But they only change for me, never for you.

# I am my own ghost, haunting the memories I love

It feels dark and lonely.
I need someone to hold me.
But I roam this empty hallway looking for a purpose.
An answer to every question I have ever wanted to ask.
All my thoughts drift away in this cold stale air surrounding me.
It makes my whole soul and what is left of my tethering body numb.
My clothes are shredded.
I am bruised and broken.
I am frozen.
I am a ghost, haunting all the memories I love.
I am a ghost, haunting my past.
Unable to let it go.
Unable to move on from this pain.

# Before Us

It was too much, too soon.
Drifting in and out of falling in love with you.
Now I do not know how I feel every time I look at you.
I do not want to, but I catch the corner of your eye from across this crowded room.
Suddenly all my old feelings for you rush back.
They flood my mind like a rising tide.
The rising tide that drowned us both,
And wrecked the love we once had.
Now it is just a memory burning in the back of my mind.
Carefully trying not to ignite the flames inside.

I wish I could go back to before us.
Before all the damage you caused,
And all the pain I had to ensue and endure from you.
I wish I could go back to the fantasy I made up in my mind.
The one that would not stop replaying.
Replaying all the moments and memories I cannot seem to forget.
At this moment, I wish for only that.
Only for the pain to stop hurting and for me to start healing.

# the masquerade

it is a crowded room,
but the only one I am looking for is you.
through the music and laughter,
everybody is dancing.
I am not dancing tonight.

you disguise yourself through fake smiles.
you have done this for a while.
you are not smiling tonight.
and I am losing you, in this crowd of people.
losing my way to all the things I wanted to be
closer to.
was it worth it, worth the pain?
if we stay like this, until we have nothing left to
say.

# Pluto

I am falling deeper everyday,
For someone who does not want me the same.
I cannot change what is done.
I cannot bring back what is gone.
It is too much pressure to put on myself.

I gave you all my thoughts.
Now I have lost my mind.
And now you have gone.
I feel so lost inside.

I am slowly moving along the shore,
As the tides all rush in.
It makes me miss you more.
I am holding onto something I will regret.
But I do not really care what happens next.

When I do not know if I want to be here anymore.
I do not know what I even want.
I have grown so used to being alone.
I do not know if I could find home in someone again.
I cannot do that to myself.
If it is only going to end,

Like everything else I know.
But lately I think I do not even know anything at all.

I come back to the same place, every night.
To ease the pain, to calm my mind.
But I still feel the same,
I still feel so empty sometimes.

I feel like I have all the weight of the world on my shoulders.
But I cannot take the weight.
Everything feels wrong.
And I do not know how much more of it I can take.
And I am worried there will be nothing left of me to save.
If I am too far gone, too far away,
Would you still want to know me?

I am floating in all the galaxies that have ever existed.
I am just Pluto from a distance.
Trying hard to make it.
But I will not make it out of here.
Out of this town.
Out of this world that will keep spinning around without me here.

I am nowhere and everywhere.
I feel nothing and everything all at once.
Until the silence comes but I still hear your echo.
It is drowning out the noise in my mind.

# Disappearing Act

I watch the cracked porcelain shatter into a
thousand pieces.
A mask so delicate, so fragile has broken.
As you watch the world being set on fire.
As the house goes up in flames.
And you cannot run from your mistakes.
Breaking slowly and painfully.
As your figure disappears into the distance.
And your memory fades into blackness.

You disappear into the shadows.
Where the darkness swallows you up.
And takes all the life from you.
Your face drained.
And skin pale.
Until every part of you is ruined.

You watch the ashes rise from the chaos and
mess you have made.
As the world falls away.
The sky turns grey.

# Silent Escape

I ran after all the things I knew I should not.
I ran until I knew I could not keep hiding,
From the shadows that mask all my demons.
Buried all in diamonds,
But my heart's been ripped open.
Now all my scars are golden,
And sown together by threads,
Of soft silk.
Marked with black ink in all the cracks and
broken pieces that used to be.
Now they are all just a memory.
Like every single thought I have ever had.
And everything I have dreamt of being but know
I will not be.

I screamed and shouted until my throat was sore
and my voice was raw.
Until I could not say a single thing anymore.
But I do not feel any better.
I have to get myself together.
And walk this long and treacherous road
With dignity.
Even if I feel like I have got none left.

# She loves to win, but she's not winning anymore

She loves to win, trying to fill a familiar
emptiness.
She drinks gin, until she cannot feel anything.
She drowns in thoughts and emotions,
That circle around in her head.
She is beautiful but she is a mess.

She loves to talk about herself.
And all the things she has done.
Everyone watches her, adores her.
Until they get bored and find someone new.
She's just old news.
On every paper, on every mat, every windowsill.
She is looking out into the world,
But never finds what she is looking for.
Searching for herself in everyone she meets.
Looking for what everyone else can see but her.
She hides behind makeup and gorgeous dresses.
Until she looks like someone else she does not
recognise at all.
She is falling hard, in all her fears.
Everything that consumes her.
Even if she does not want to fall.

She runs from afraid,
And hides from all her confusion.
Trying to be brave, holding onto her.
Holding onto something.
She clings onto anything that reminds her of her past.
The one she loves to be in.
The one that makes her feel like herself.
But that is not her anymore.
Just a figment now.
Just a memory of everything she used to be.

And she hates it.
When the lights dim.
She is left alone with all her feelings.
She aches inside her whole being.
Shaking from exhaustion and overthinking.
She does not know how to process her grief,
At losing the only part of her she ever loved.

# Firebird

Like diamonds fashioned from the rubble and dirt,
I am beautiful.
Covered in jewels to mask the brokenness of my soul and everything inside me.

Like a firebird.
I soar across scorched islands,
And glide along riverbeds.
My sparks ignite with one touch.
And I get caught in the fire that burns from my wings,
When I run into the dark.
Alone and preoccupied.
With foreign thoughts and emotions.
My mind runs wild at night.
Everything escapes me.

I release all my fears into the open.
Imagining myself walking into the bridge of life and death.
Hanging on the side of a lonely cliff above me,
The ropes cling onto me,
Broken and untied.
Fragmented and secluded.

The rocks that sit beside me,
Sink into the cold water below.
Drowning in its depth.

I imagine myself floating in its capacity once I reach the end.
The end before the drop.
Testing my ability to float, rather than drown.
I edge closer to the deep end,
Trying my best not to sink.
The water pulls me along.
And I allow myself to drift away with the tide.
Falling at its feet.

Finally free.
Finally coping.

www.ingramcontent.com/pod-product-compliance
Lightning Source LLC
Chambersburg PA
CBHW051745130826
49812CB00033B/1014
* 9 7 8 9 3 5 7 2 1 2 6 7 0 *